TIMOTHY KNAPMAN   NIK HENDERSON

THE BOOK OF BLAST OFF!

15 real-life SPACE missions

MAGIC CAT 🐱 PUBLISHING

NEW YORK

I'm looking out my window
at the dark and twinkling sky.
It's full of stars and planets
and bright comets *whooshing* by.

Quick, I hear the countdown!
Let's get into position . . .
Come with me, and let's go on
an interstellar mission!

Five . . .

Four . . .

Three . . .

Two . . .

One . . .

BLAST OFF!

SPUTNIK 1, the satellite,
was first to orbit **Earth**.
It sent out radio signals
for all that it was worth.

heat shield

antenna

Its mission lasted three short weeks,
and then its job was done,
but it started something serious . . .
The
GREAT SPACE RACE
was *on!*

Although Yuri Gagarin
was the first in outer space,
the launch of **FRIENDSHIP 7**
put the U.S. in the race.

heat shield

rocket engine

second stage

first stage

John Glenn circled **Earth** three times,
he saw our planet glow,

antenna

and looking up, he knew there was
much farther we could go.

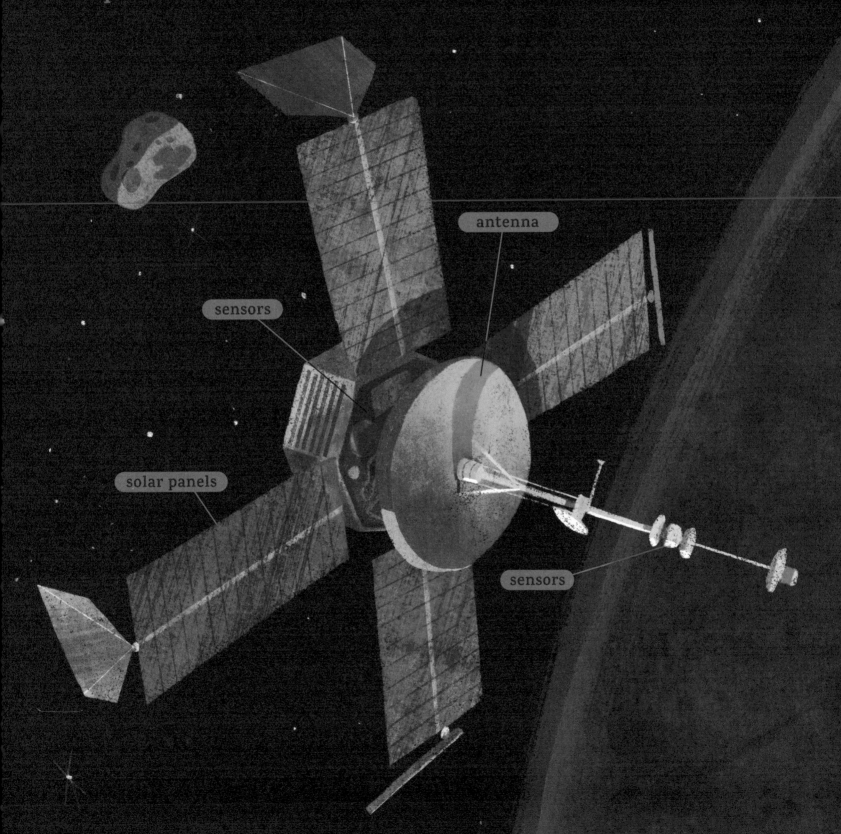

MARINER 4 was sent to see
if there was life on **Mars**.
It took a lot of pictures
of a planet full of scars . . .

antenna

sensors

solar panels

sensors

Craters made by meteoroids,
a world with such thin air.

But still the search goes on
to see if life exists out there.

Neil Armstrong and Buzz Aldrin
landed **EAGLE** on the moon.
Once they'd shown it could be done,
we knew we'd be back soon.

antenna

antenna

thrust chamber

landing gear

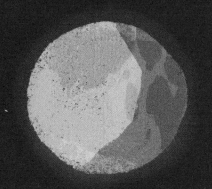

One small step for Armstrong
was one giant leap for all.
From here, they stood admiring Earth—
our precious blue-green ball.

The **APOLLO 13** moonshot
gave us all a dreadful scare:

a tank of gas **exploded!**
Soon the crew would have no air!

propulsion system

antenna

heat shield

The world watched as they racked their brains
and found ways to survive.
The mission was abandoned,
but they all came home alive.

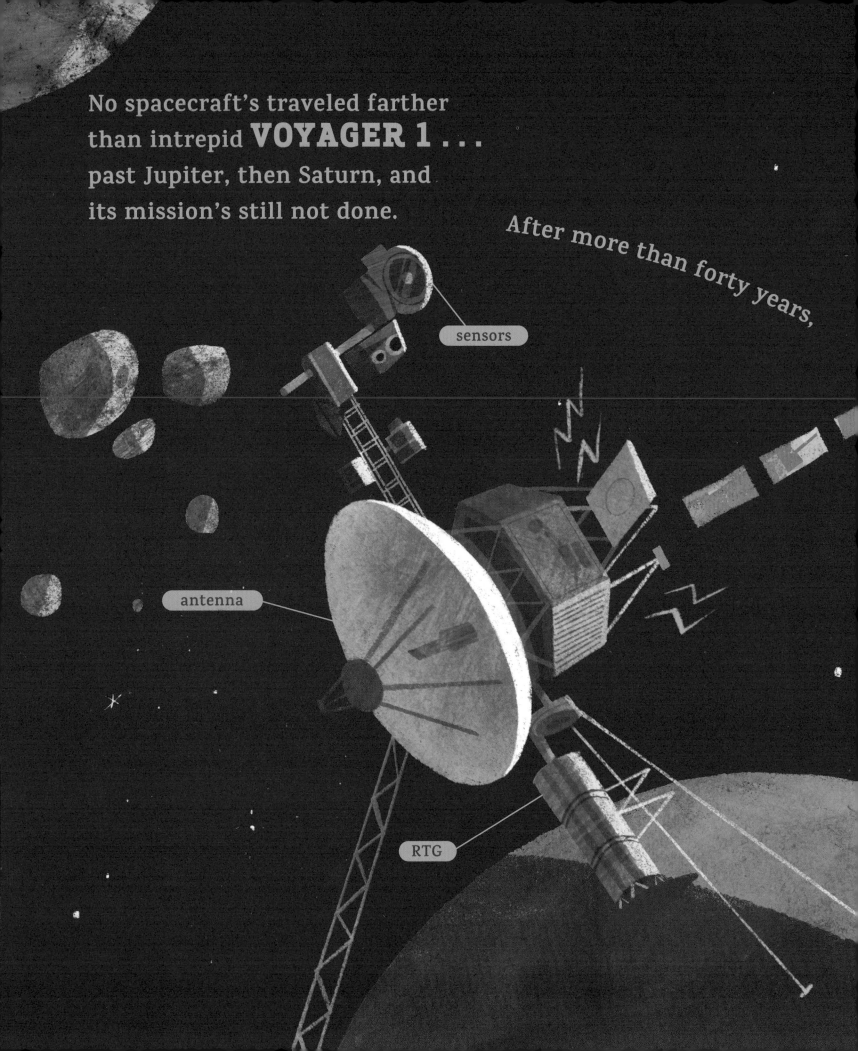

No spacecraft's traveled farther than intrepid **VOYAGER 1** . . . past Jupiter, then Saturn, and its mission's still not done.

After more than forty years,

sensors

antenna

RTG

it still calls home today . . . .

even though it's over
fourteen billion miles away!

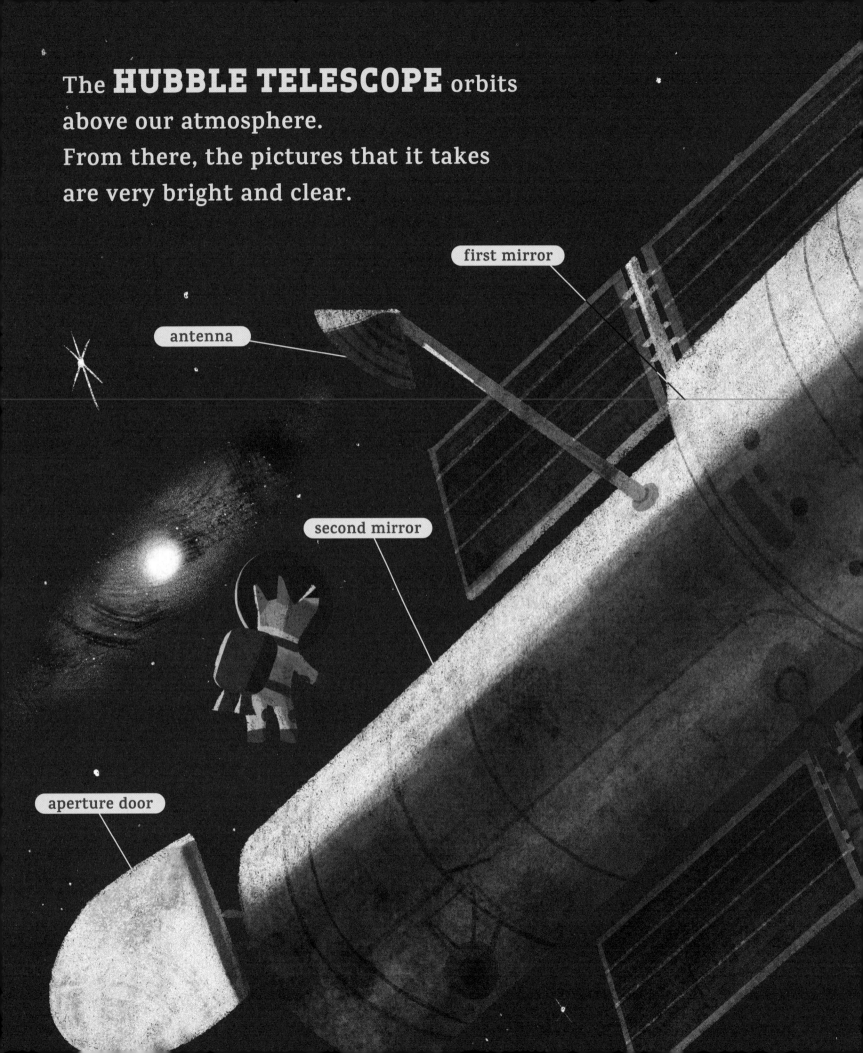

The **HUBBLE TELESCOPE** orbits
above our atmosphere.
From there, the pictures that it takes
are very bright and clear.

first mirror

antenna

second mirror

aperture door

The **DISCOVERY** crew released it in the perfect place, and now, because of Hubble, we can see deep into space.

solar panels

Round **Jupiter** the giant, clouds
of gas and questions swirled.
So off went **GALILEO**
to investigate this world.

RTG

sun shield

antenna

It spent eight years in orbit,
looked at asteroids as well,
and dropped a probe to the planet
that sent data as it fell.

CASSINI-HUYGENS traveled
to see **Saturn** and its rings.
It spotted several brand new moons
and more amazing things . . .

antenna

engines

RTG

sensor

It saw flashes of lightning
and a most unusual storm
that looked like a hurricane
with a strange, six-sided form.

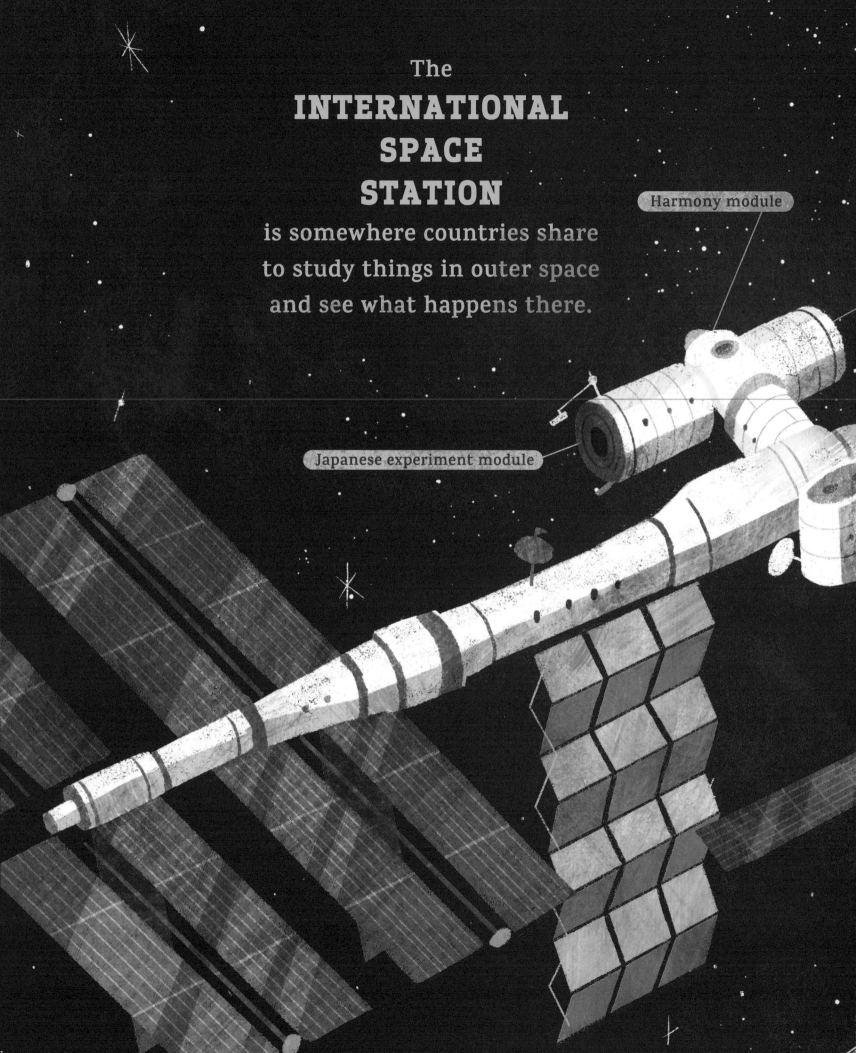

The
INTERNATIONAL
SPACE
STATION
is somewhere countries share
to study things in outer space
and see what happens there.

Harmony module

Japanese experiment module

solar panels

Columbus module

service module

The ISS is very big,
with room for all its crew,
and every day it orbits **Earth**.
Look up—it might pass you!

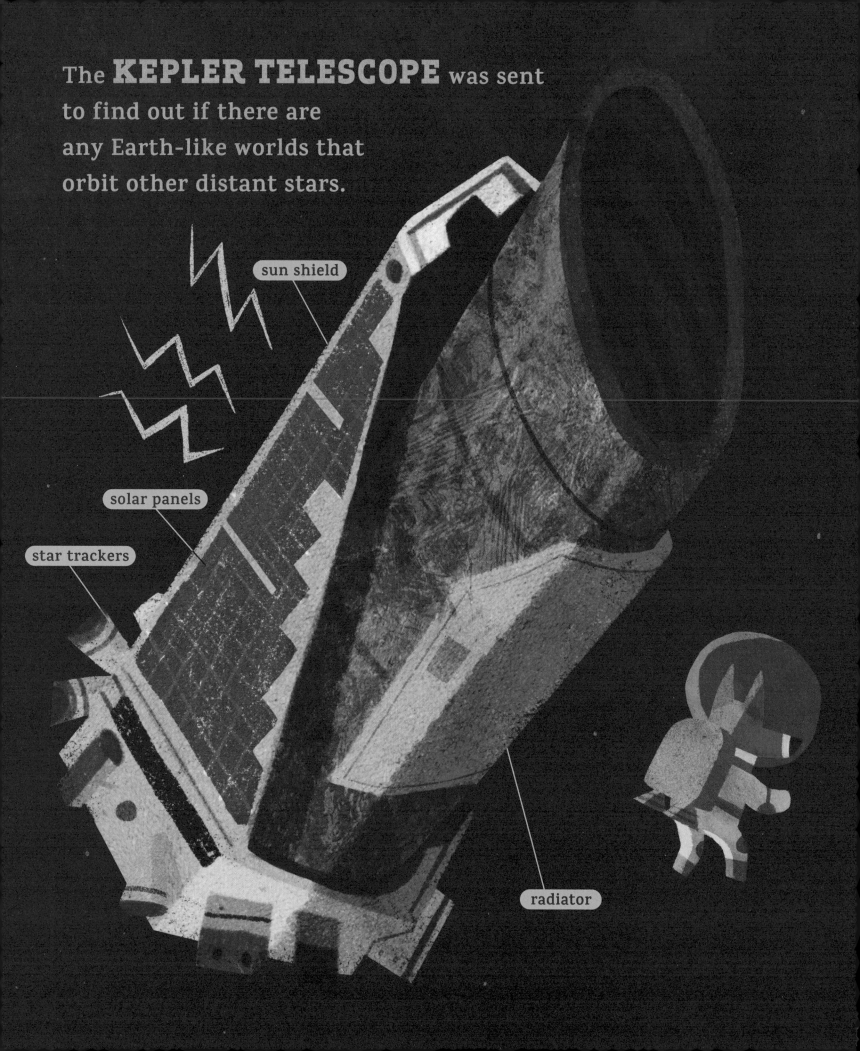

The **KEPLER TELESCOPE** was sent to find out if there are any Earth-like worlds that orbit other distant stars.

sun shield

solar panels

star trackers

radiator

Before its mission ended,
it discovered, if you wondered,
several Earth-sized planets—
in fact, more than one hundred!

Comets are **huge** chunks of ice
and rock that zoom around.
The probe **ROSETTA** went to see
a comet that we'd found.

It took a look from orbit and, wanting to explore,
sent down the lander **PHILAE**

scientific instruments

sensors

drill

so that it could

learn some more.

Jessica Meir flew to the **ISS**,
with her friend Christina Koch.
There was a problem with the power . . .
so they went out to take a look.

As the pair worked, folks back on Earth
shared much excited talk,
welcoming this special first:
an **all-female spacewalk!**

There's no life on **Mars** right now,
but was there long ago?
We sent a new machine
to see what there is to know . . .

The **PERSEVERANCE ROVER**
(known as Percy to his friends)
confirmed Mars once had water—
upon which all life depends.

cameras

scientific instruments

navigation sensors

We're going to the **moon** again.

This time it is to stay.

We'll have a gateway up in space—
a moon base too, someday.

TO OUTER SPACE ...
AND BEYOND!

Since ancient humans first looked up into the night sky, we've wondered about space and wanted to travel there. But it's only in our relatively recent history that space exploration turned from a dream into a reality.

The first human-made object was sent into space in 1957. This marked the beginning of frenzied activity on Earth to travel faster and farther into space, reimagining the limits of what humans could achieve, over and over again.

Here's a little more information about some of these iconic missions.

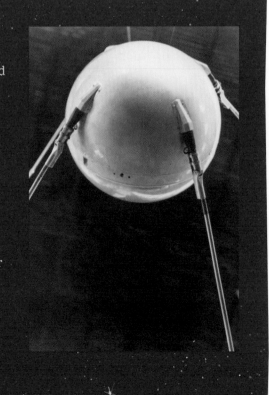

The Space Race
Date: 1957–1969

The Soviet Union existed from 1922 until 1991 and spanned across eastern Europe and northern Asia. Its capital was Moscow, now part of Russia. In the years following World War II, the Soviet Union and the United States were two of the world's most powerful nations, but they disagreed about many things. The tension between the two is often called the Cold War. In 1957, the United States was shocked to learn that the Soviet Union had succeeded in launching the first satellite. Soon all eyes turned to the moon . . . and who would be the first one there. Would it be a Russian cosmonaut or an American astronaut? The race was on.

Mission: Sputnik 1
Date: October 4, 1957

When Sputnik 1 was launched into orbit by the Soviet Union, it became the first human-made object in space. Sputnik means "fellow traveler" in Russian. The satellite was small—the size of a beach ball—and featured several long antennae. Expected to run out of battery power in just two weeks, Sputnik continued transmitting radio signals for twenty-two days . . . and its legacy lasted much longer. The age of space exploration had begun.

Mission: Vostok 1
Date: April 12, 1961
Crew: Yuri A. Gagarin

Soviet cosmonaut Yuri Gagarin launched into history aboard *Vostok 1*, becoming the first human to orbit Earth. The spacecraft had a round cabin and three small portholes, and Gagarin communicated with ground personnel by radio during the flight. *Vostok* orbited Earth once and landed an hour and forty-eight minutes after it launched. As planned, Gagarin ejected himself from the craft about four miles above Earth and landed by parachute. He touched down in a field, startling a farmer and her granddaughter.

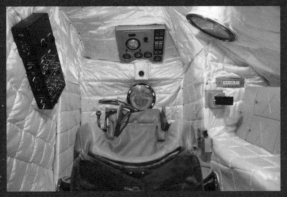

Mission: Mercury-Atlas 6
Date: February 20, 1962
Crew: John H. Glenn Jr.

John Glenn became the first American to orbit Earth during the Mercury-Atlas 6 mission. Launched from atop an eight-story-tall Atlas booster rocket, the *Friendship 7* spacecraft circled Earth three times. Glenn observed a dust storm in Africa, the glow of moonlight on the ocean and clouds, and four sunsets. When the autopilot function failed, Glenn took over the manual controls and completed the nearly five-hour flight before successfully splashing down in the Atlantic Ocean.

Mission: Mariner 4
Date: November 28, 1964

Weighing 575 pounds and powered by four solar panels, Mariner 4 successfully completed the first flyby of Mars. Launched from Cape Canaveral, Florida, the craft traveled for seven months before reaching its closest approach to Mars on July 15, 1965. It captured the first photographs of another planet from deep space. The photos dashed any hopes of discovering life on the Red Planet, but the mission deepened our understanding of Mars.

Mission: Apollo 11, Moon Landing
Date: July 16–24, 1969
Crew: Neil A. Armstrong, Edwin E. "Buzz" Aldrin Jr., Michael Collins

On July 20, 1969, some 650 million people tuned in to watch the historic moon landing. Apollo 11's Lunar Module *Eagle* separated from the main command module, piloted by Michael Collins, and descended to the moon's surface. American astronaut Neil Armstrong became the first person to walk on the moon. He famously declared, "That's one small step for a man, one giant leap for mankind." Armstrong and Aldrin spent over twenty-one hours on the moon before *Eagle* docked with the command module and returned to Earth.

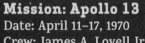

Mission: Voyager
Date: September 5, 1977–

Launched in 1977, *Voyager 1* is still going. It explored Jupiter in 1979 and Saturn in 1980, collecting tens of thousands of images and measurements along with its counterpart, *Voyager 2*. Today, it's the farthest human-made object from Earth. In August 2012, it became the first spacecraft to reach interstellar space—a part of space so far away that it lies beyond the sun's atmosphere—and it is still sending data back to Earth. *Voyager 1* carries a copy of the Golden Record, a message for any alien life forms it might encounter on its journey.

Mission: Apollo 13
Date: April 11–17, 1970
Crew: James A. Lovell Jr., John L. "Jack" Swigert Jr., Fred W. Haise Jr.

Apollo 13 was supposed to be the third mission to the moon. But fifty-six hours into the flight, an oxygen tank exploded. The systems that provided the crew's air and the ship's electric power were badly damaged. The crew was in grave danger. The moon landing was canceled and an emergency plan was hatched. The astronauts moved into the ship's cramped lunar lander, which served as their lifeboat, supplying them with enough air, water, and power to make it home.

Mission: STS-31, Space Shuttle *Discovery*, Hubble Launch

Date: April 24–29, 1990
Crew: Loren J. Shriver, Charles F. Bolden Jr.,
Steven A. Hawley, Bruce McCandless II,
Kathryn D. Sullivan

The National Aeronautics and Space Administration (NASA), designs space shuttles that can be used for multiple missions. Five shuttles completed 135 missions from 1981 to 2011. During the STS-31 mission, Space Shuttle Discovery launched the Hubble Space Telescope. Able to detect the most distant and faint objects we had ever studied (until the James Webb Space Telescope began sending data in 2022), Hubble has offered us views of black holes, planets that orbit distant stars, and other cosmic wonders. It is still in operation today. In 2009, STS-31's pilot, Charles F. Bolden Jr., was named administrator of NASA, becoming the first Black American to hold the agency's top spot.

Mission: Galileo

Date: October 18, 1989–September 21, 2003

While traveling to Jupiter, *Galileo* became the first spacecraft to encounter an asteroid, flying very close to two of them. The craft orbited Jupiter for seven years, nine months, and made exciting discoveries about Jupiter's moons, finding evidence of a saltwater ocean beneath the ice on Europa and widespread volcanic eruptions on Io. A probe released from the craft took readings of Jupiter's atmosphere and showed that Jupiter has massive thunderstorms, much stronger than those on Earth. *Galileo* ended transmissions in 2003 after scientists deliberately crashed it into Jupiter.

Mission: Cassini-Huygens

Date: October 15, 1997–September 15, 2017

The robotic spacecraft *Cassini* orbited Saturn, exploring its famous rings and dozens of icy moons, and witnessing its massive storms. It also carried a probe called *Huygens* that parachuted down to Saturn's moon Titan, where it found evidence of ice volcanoes and collected other data. *Cassini* traveled 4.9 billion miles and sent back more than 450,000 images that show the wonders of Saturn. NASA, the European Space Agency, and Agenzia Spaziale (the Italian Space Agency), worked together on the Cassini mission.

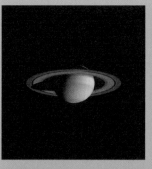

Mission: **Expedition 1, International Space Station**
Date: October 31, 2000–March 21, 2001
Crew: William M. Shepherd, Sergei K. Krikalev, Yuri P. Gidzenko

In 1993, the United States and Russia agreed to work together to create the International Space Station (ISS), a state-of-the-art space lab. Once the space station was ready to receive astronauts for a long-term stay, one American and two Russians blasted off from Kazakhstan and arrived at the ISS on November 2, 2000. After four months, the crew returned to Earth on the Space Shuttle *Discovery*, which had dropped off a new ISS crew. The International Space Station has been continually occupied since 2000 and is operated by an international partnership that includes the United States, Europe, Japan, and Canada.

Mission: **Kepler**
Date: March 7, 2009–November 15, 2018

How many Earth-sized planets lie beyond our solar system? Could any of them have the right conditions for life? The Kepler space telescope was launched to begin to answer those questions. It observed more than 500,000 stars, searching for changes in brightness that could indicate a planet nearby. If a planet was detected, Kepler could gather data to estimate the planet's size, orbit, and surface temperature. To date, Kepler has identified 2,711 confirmed exoplanets—planets found outside our solar system—and a hundred or so Earth-sized worlds.

Mission: **Rosetta and Philae**
Date: 2 March, 2004–30 September, 2016

The European Space Agency's Rosetta and Philae mission was the first to orbit and land on a comet. The Rosetta spacecraft followed Comet 67P/Churyumov-Gerasimenko as it orbited the sun and released the Philae space probe to land on its surface. Unfortunately, the landing didn't go as planned. Philae bounced and came to rest in a spot too dark to charge its batteries, but it sent back important data before it lost power. Rosetta continued on for another two years—collecting and analyzing samples and sending back photos and data that have changed our understanding of comets.

Glossary

antenna—a rod or structure that can receive and/or transmit radio waves

aperture door—a door that can be closed to prevent light from the Sun from causing any damage to a telecope or its instruments

heat shield—a system that protects against extremely high temperatures

first stage—part of the spacecraft that ignites at launch, providing the main thrust to make liftoff from Earth possible, before emptying and falling away

landing gear—equipment that allows a spacecraft to liftoff and/or land safely by providing suspension

light meter—an instrument that measures light

module—a self-contained unit of a spacecraft; each module has its own purpose

navigation sensors—scientific instruments that help a rover move safely across terrain

propulsion system—a system that produces thrust to push a spacecraft forward

RTG—abbreviation of "radioisotope thermoelectric generator": a nuclear battery that converts heat energy into electrical power

second stage—once the first stage of a spacecraft drops away, the second stage takes over and provides thrust, before it, too, empties and falls away

solar panel—a device that converts energy from light into electricity

thrust chamber—an assembly that allows a spacecraft to move in space by spraying out gas

weather station—scientific instruments that collect data about weather and climate

Further Reading

The Darkest Dark
by Chris Hadfield, illustrated by the Fan Brothers

Hidden Figures: The True Story of Four Black Women and the Space Race
by Margot Lee Shetterly, illustrated by Laura Freeman

Moonshot: The Flight of Apollo 11
by Brian Floca

This Is the Way to the Moon
by Miroslav Sasek

The depictions of spacecraft in this book are an artist's impression and have in some places been simplified to make them appropriate for a younger readership.

PHOTO CREDITS

Space Race: NASA; **Sputnik 1:** NASA; **Vostok 1:** Art_rich/Shutterstock (top), yakub88/Shutterstock (left); Gilmanshin/Shutterstock (right); **Mercury-Atlas 6:** NASA (both); **Mariner 4:** NASA; **Apollo 11:** NASA (all); **Apollo 13:** NASA; **Voyager 1:** NASA; **Mission STS-31:** NASA; **Galileo:** NASA (both); **Cassini-Huygens:** NASA/JPL/Space Science Institute (top left), ESA-C. Carreau (top right), NASA/JPL-Caltech (bottom); **Expedition 1:** NASA (all); **Kepler:** NASA; **Rosetta and Philae:** ESA-J. Huart, 2013; **Expedition 61:** NASA/Robert Markowitz (left), NASA (right); **Perseverance:** NASA/JPL-Caltech/MSSS; **Artemis:** NASA (both); **Rosetta and Philae:** ESA-J. Huart; **Expedition 61:** NASA/Robert Markowitz (top), NASA (bottom); **Perseverance:** NASA/JPL-Caltech/MSSS; **Artemis:** NASA (both)

To Peter, with love—T.K.
For my parents, and the aspiring little astronauts and astronomers—N.H.

MAGIC CAT PUBLISHING

The illustrations in this book were created digitally. Set in Karma and Apex.

Library of Congress Control Number 2022944490

ISBN 978-1-4197-6595-7

Text © 2023 Timothy Knapman
Illustrations © 2023 Nik Henderson
Cover © 2023 Magic Cat
Book design by Stephanie Jones and Ella Tomkins

First published in North America in 2023 by Magic Cat Publishing, an imprint of ABRAMS. First published in the United Kingdom in 2023 by Magic Cat Publishing Ltd. All rights reserved. No portion of this book may be reproduced, stored in a retrieval system, or transmitted in any form or by any means, mechanical, electronic, photocopying, recording, or otherwise, without written permission from the publisher.

Printed and bound in China
10 9 8 7 6 5 4 3 2 1

Abrams Books are available at special discounts when purchased in quantity for premiums and promotions as well as fundraising or educational use. Special editions can also be created to specification. For details, contact specialsales@abramsbooks.com or the address below.

ABRAMS The Art of Books
195 Broadway, New York, NY 10007
abramsbooks.com

Mission: Expedition 61, International Space Station
Date: October 3, 2019–February 6, 2020
Crew: Andrew R. Morgan, Aleksandr Skvortsov, Luca Parmitano, Oleg Skripochka, Jessica U. Meir, Christina H. Koch

During their seven-hour, seventeen-minute spacewalk on October 18, 2019, Christina Koch and Jessica Meir changed a power unit . . . and made history. The 221st spacewalk at the International Space Station was the first spacewalk ever to be performed by an all-female team. Meir and Koch join a long list of women leading the way in the space program. Some notable female astronauts include Russian cosmonaut Valentina Tereshkova, the first woman in space; Sally Ride, the first American woman in space; Mae Jemison, the first Black woman in space; and Peggy Whitson, who spent a record-setting 665 days in space.

Mission: Mars 2020, *Perseverance*
Date: July 30, 2020–

Mars may not be home to Martians, but the *Perseverance* rover was sent to explore a site that was known to once feature a deep lake and rushing river. Since landing on the Red Planet in 2021, "Percy" has collected rock samples that will be brought back to Earth on a future Mars Sample Return mission. The car-sized rover has cameras and instruments to help it "see," antennas for communicating, a "hand" for collecting samples, and wheels and legs for getting around. A helicopter called *Ingenuity* is being used to explore areas around the landing site.

Mission: Artemis
Date: Coming soon!

Would you live on the moon? NASA's upcoming Artemis missions will explore more of the moon's surface and establish a base camp on the moon where astronauts can live and work. NASA has announced that it will land the first woman and person of color on the moon during these missions. Using what they learn, NASA hopes to one day send astronauts to Mars!

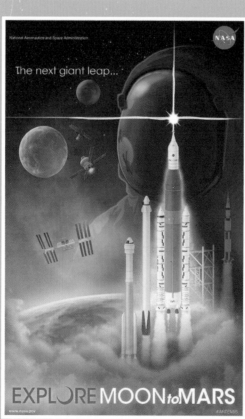